What's the Bill of Rights?

Revised Edition

Nancy Harris

capstone

©2008, 2016 Heinemann Library
an imprint of Capstone Global Library, LLC. Chicago, Illinois

To contact Capstone Global Library, please
call 800-747-4992, or visit our web site
www.capstonepub.com

Editorial: Rebecca Rissman
Design: Kimberly R. Miracle and Betsy Wernert
Illustrations: Mapping Specialists
Photo Research: Tracy Cummins and Heather Mauldin
Production: Duncan Gilbert

**Library of Congress Cataloging-in-Publication Data
is available on the Library of Congress website.**
    ISBN 978-1-4846-3689-3 (revised paperback)
    ISBN 978-1-4846-3495-0 (ebook)

Image Credits
AP Photo: 17, Alex Brandon, 19; Capstone Press: Mapping Specialists, 8, 25; Corbis: Bettmann/Joe Marquette, 26; Dreamstime: Americanspirit, 29; Getty Images: Alex Wong, 16, Scott J. Ferrell, 27; iStockphoto: CastaldoStudio, 7, 15, 24; Library of Congress: 9; National Archives and Records Administration: 4, 6; Newscom: Picture History, 12; North Wind Picture Archives: 11, 13; Shutterstock: bikeriderlondon, 20, 22, Dennis Steen, 18, Everett Historical, 14 Right, 14 Left, Rena Schild, 5, wavebreakmedia, 23; Thinkstock: AlexanderDonchev, Cover, Chip Somodevilla, 28, Photos.com, 10, Stockbyte, 21
Cover image used with permission of ©Getty (Craig Brewer).

The publishers would like to thank Nancy Harris for her assistance in the preparation of this book.
Every effort has been made to contact copyright holders of any material reproduced in this book. Any omissions will be rectified in subsequent printings if notice is given to the publisher.

Table of Contents

Some words are shown in bold, **like this**. You can find out what they mean by looking in the glossary.

What Is the Bill of Rights?

The Bill of Rights is part of the U.S. Constitution. The Constitution is a very important **document** (paper). It is a written **law** (rule) that must be obeyed by everyone in the United States.

★ This is the U.S. Constitution.

★ The Bill of Rights gives Americans the freedom of speech.

The Bill of Rights protects the **rights** of people who live in the United States. Rights are freedoms that people have. Rights include how people are treated and what they can do. Some of the rights that are protected include the right to say and write what you think.

The U.S. Constitution

The U.S. Constitution has three parts. The first part is the **preamble**. This section tells why the Constitution was written. The second part is the **articles**. These create the **federal government** and describe how it works. The federal government leads the country.

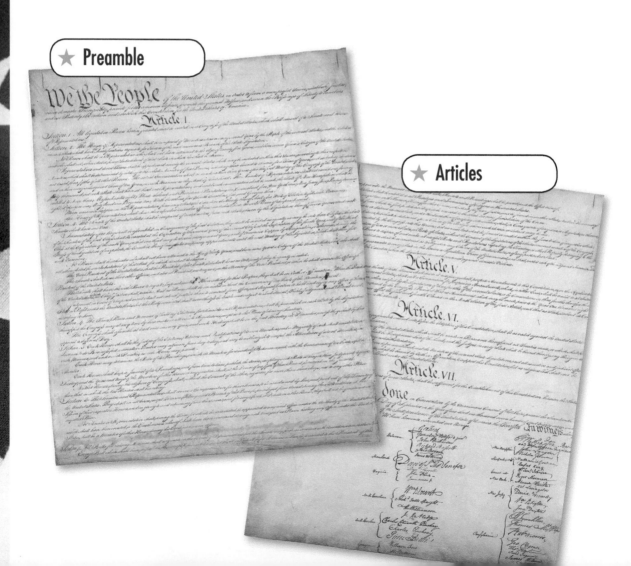

★ Preamble

★ Articles

The third part of the Constitution is made up of **amendments**. These are changes or additions that have been made to the Constitution since it was first written. These changes are new **laws**. The Bill of Rights is the first 10 amendments.

The Bill of Rights was written in 1789. It was added to the Constitution two years later.

7

History of the Constitution

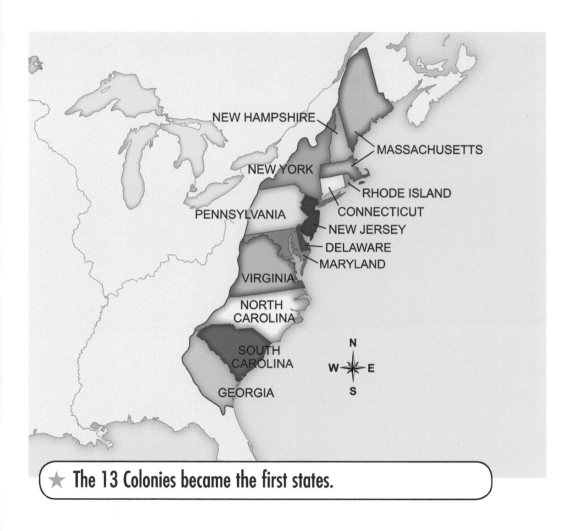

NEW HAMPSHIRE

MASSACHUSETTS

NEW YORK

RHODE ISLAND

CONNECTICUT

PENNSYLVANIA

NEW JERSEY

DELAWARE

MARYLAND

VIRGINIA

NORTH CAROLINA

SOUTH CAROLINA

GEORGIA

★ The 13 Colonies became the first states.

The U.S. Constitution was written in 1787. The United States was still a new country. There were only 13 states. The people who lived there had fought hard to become a new country.

The people had fought against Great Britain. At that time, the states were called **colonies**. A colony is a place people move to from another country. The people who lived there were called **colonists**. The king of Great Britain ruled the colonists.

⭐ American colonists fought a war against Great Britain.

★ The colonists were ruled by King George the Third.

The **colonists** did not like living under British rule. The king had taken away many of the colonists' rights. The colonists could not decide how they would be punished if they broke a law. They were not allowed to meet in groups to discuss things.

The colonists met to decide how the United States should be ruled.

This made the colonists unhappy. When they became a new country, they wanted their rights protected. They decided that their rights needed to be part of the Constitution.

Adding the Bill of Rights

The Constitution created the **federal government** and explained how it would work. The authors of the Constitution wanted to make sure that no part of the government had too much power. They wanted to protect the new country from being ruled by one leader.

★ Important leaders helped to write the Constitution.

★★★ Only 10 of the first 12 amendments became the Bill of Rights.

The group of men wrote 12 **amendments** to the Constitution. Amendments can only be added if people in the **federal government** and **state governments** vote in favor of them. People voted to add 10 of these amendments to the Constitution.

The Bill of Rights

These ten **amendments** became the first amendments to the Constitution and make up the Bill of Rights. They were added to the Constitution in 1791. This was just four years after the Constitution had been written.

★ You can view the Bill of Rights in Washington, D.C.

★★★ The First Amendment allowed Martin Luther King, Jr. to give his "I Have a Dream" speech.

The First Amendment

The First Amendment says that people have a right to meet and discuss things. People have the right to believe in the religion of their choice. People have the right to say and write what they think.

The Bill of Rights gives this person the right to own a gun.

The Second and Third Amendments

The Second **Amendment** says that people have the right to own weapons, such as guns. They have a right to protect themselves.

The Third Amendment says that soldiers do not have the right to stay in people's homes without permission. In the past, soldiers had stayed in people's homes without their permission.

The Fourth Amendment

The Fourth Amendment says that people's houses and belongings are private. Police cannot search people's homes without permission. Police also cannot take people's belongings without permission.

★ Police need permission to search homes.

The Fifth Amendment says that the police must treat people fairly.

The Fifth Amendment

The Fifth **Amendment** describes how people can be **accused** of a crime. This amendment also protects people from having to speak against themselves if they are accused of breaking a law.

★ Lawyers help people defend themselves in court.

The Sixth Amendment

The Sixth Amendment says that people have a right to be defended by a **lawyer** if they are accused of a crime. A lawyer is a person who knows and understands the law.

The Seventh Amendment

The Seventh **Amendment** says that people have a right to a **jury trial** if they are accused of breaking a law. A **jury** is a group of people who have been chosen to decide if a **law** has been broken. They listen to each side before making a decision.

★ A jury can decide if a crime has been committed.

★ Lawyers and judges make sure people are treated fairly.

The Eighth Amendment

The Eighth Amendment says that people have the right to fair treatment. People must be given a fair punishment if it is decided that they have broken a law. The punishment must not be unfair or too harsh.

The Ninth Amendment

The Ninth **Amendment** says that people have rights that cannot be taken away from them. Some of these rights are not listed in the Constitution. This amendment was added so the government could not take away any rights that are not listed in the Constitution.

★ The Ninth Amendment protects people's rights.

The Tenth Amendment

The Tenth Amendment says that each state in the United States has rights that cannot be taken away from that state. These rights include how each **state government** leads the state. Each state must also obey the laws of the federal government.

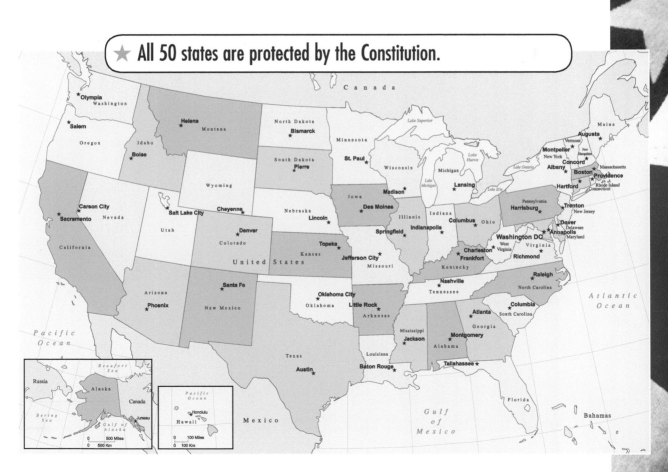

★ All 50 states are protected by the Constitution.

Other Amendments

★★★ Leaders must convince the government to accept an amendment.

Other **amendments** have been added to the Constitution. There are currently 27 amendments. The 27th Amendment was added in 1992.

★ These lawmakers work to make the United States better.

The Constitution can be **amended** (changed) at any time. The new **laws** are made to meet the needs of people in the United States. They are made to protect people's rights.

Why Is the Bill of Rights Important?

The Bill of Rights makes sure that people in the United States are all treated the same way. It protects people from being treated harshly by a government or leader. It makes sure they are treated fairly.

★ New citizens are protected by the Bill of Rights.

★ The Constitution is on display in Washington, D.C.

The Bill of Rights is an important part of the U.S. Constitution. It protects the rights of people in the United States.

Glossary

accuse state that someone has committed a crime or broken a law

amend change a piece of text. You can amend the constitution by adding a new law, which is called an amendment.

amendment change made to a piece of writing. The change could be a text change or something that has been added to the text. An amendment to the Constitution is when you add a new law.

article part or piece of writing in a text. There are articles in the U.S. Constitution.

colonists people who live in a colony

colony place people move to from another country. A colony is ruled or led by the country the people moved from.

document written text or paper. The U.S. Constitution is a document.

federal government group of leaders who run the entire country. In a federal government, the country is made up of many states.

jury group of people selected to decide whether someone has broken a law

jury trial when a group of people on a jury listen in a court to decide if a law has been broken. A court is a place where people go if they are accused of breaking a law.

law rule people must obey in a state or country

lawyer person who knows the law. Lawyers help people who go to court. They try to get the jury to agree with that person's opinion.

preamble first part of a text. It explains why the paper was written.

rights freedoms that people have. Rights include the right to say and write what you think.

state government group of leaders who run a state. Each state in the United States has a state government.

Find Out More

Books to Read

An older reader can help you with these books:

Hamilton, John. *The Bill of Rights*. Edina, MN: Abdo Publishing, 2005.

Krull, Kathleen. *Kids Guide to America's Bill of Rights*. New York: Harper Collins, 1999.

Pearl, Norman. *The Bill of Rights*. Mankato, MN: Picture Window Books, 2007.

Internet Sites

FactHound offers a safe, fun way to find Internet sites related to this book. All of the sites on FactHound have been researched by our staff

Visit www.fachound.com

Viewing the U.S. Constitution

The U.S. Constitution is on display in the National Archives in the Rotunda. The Rotunda is open daily from 9 am to 5 pm.

The National Archives address is:
700 Pennsylvania Avenue, NW
Washington, D.C. 20408

Index